A Comprehensive Overview of Global Challenges

C. P. Kumar
Reiki Healer
Roorkee - 247667, India

DEDICATION

Dedicated to all those who have experienced the impact of global challenges, this book aims to shed light on the pressing issues faced by humanity today.

To those who have suffered the consequences of climate change, income inequality, discrimination, displacement, and other challenges, this book is dedicated to providing a comprehensive overview of the root causes, consequences, and possible solutions to these complex issues.

We dedicate this book to all those who strive to create a better world, to those who work tirelessly to promote equality, justice, and sustainable development for all.

This book is dedicated to inspiring positive change, empowering individuals and communities to take action, and building a brighter future for generations to come.

C. P. Kumar

CONTENTS

PREFACE

As our world becomes increasingly interconnected, we face a multitude of challenges that impact our global community. From climate change to political polarization, the issues we face are complex, multifaceted, and interrelated. This book, "A Comprehensive Overview of Global Challenges," seeks to provide a broad understanding of these challenges and offer insights into potential solutions.

The book is divided into 15 chapters, each focusing on a particular global challenge that affects individuals and societies around the world. These challenges include climate change and environmental degradation, income inequality and poverty, access to quality education and healthcare, political polarization and division, discrimination and prejudice based on race, gender, religion, and sexual orientation, cybersecurity and privacy concerns, increasing levels of debt and financial instability, displacement of people due to war, conflict, and natural disasters, global pandemics and public health crises, nuclear weapons proliferation and the threat of war, corruption and lack of transparency in government and corporations, food insecurity and malnutrition, aging population and declining birth rates in some regions, lack of affordable housing and rising homelessness, and addiction and mental health issues.

The aim of this book is to provide readers with a comprehensive understanding of these issues, their causes and effects, and potential solutions. Each chapter explores the latest research and data on the topic, as well as case studies and real-world examples that illustrate the impact of these global challenges. The book also examines the roles of various stakeholders, including governments, non-governmental organizations, corporations, and individuals, in addressing these challenges.

This book is intended for a broad audience, including policymakers, academics, students, and anyone interested in gaining a deeper understanding of the global challenges we face today. We hope that this book will serve as a valuable resource for readers, inspiring new ideas and solutions to the complex issues that affect our world.

C. P. Kumar
Reiki Healer
Former Scientist 'G', National Institute of Hydrology
Roorkee - 247667, India
E-mail: cpkumar@yahoo.com
Web: https://www.angelfire.com/nh/cpkumar/virgo.html

Introduction

Climate change and environmental degradation are two interconnected global challenges that have emerged as some of the biggest threats to human existence. Climate change refers to the long-term alteration of temperature and weather patterns on Earth, which is largely caused by human activities such as the burning of fossil fuels, deforestation, and industrial processes. Environmental degradation, on the other hand, refers to the deterioration of the natural environment due to human activities such as pollution, overconsumption of resources, and habitat destruction. These two issues are intertwined, as the degradation of the environment contributes to climate change, and climate change, in turn, exacerbates environmental degradation. In this article, we will explore the causes, impacts, and potential solutions to climate change and environmental degradation.

Causes of Climate Change and Environmental Degradation

Human activities are the primary cause of climate change and environmental degradation. The burning of fossil fuels, such as coal, oil, and gas, releases large amounts of carbon dioxide and other greenhouse gases into the atmosphere, trapping heat and causing global temperatures to rise. Deforestation, which involves the clearing of forests for agriculture, logging, and other purposes, also contributes to climate change by reducing the number of trees that absorb carbon dioxide from the atmosphere. Industrial processes, transportation, and agriculture are also major sources of greenhouse gas emissions.

Environmental degradation is caused by a range of human activities, including pollution, overconsumption of resources, and habitat destruction. Pollution can take many forms, such as air pollution from factories and transportation, water pollution from industrial and agricultural runoff, and soil pollution from toxic chemicals. Overconsumption of resources, such as water, food, and energy, can lead to the depletion of natural resources and the destruction of ecosystems. Habitat destruction, such as deforestation and urbanization, can lead to the loss of biodiversity and the disruption of ecological systems.

Impacts of Climate Change and Environmental Degradation

Climate change and environmental degradation have a range of impacts on human health, ecosystems, and economies. Climate change has led to rising sea levels, more frequent and severe weather events, and the loss of biodiversity. Rising temperatures and changing weather patterns also have a range of impacts on human health, including increased incidence of heat-related illnesses and respiratory diseases. Environmental degradation has led to the loss of biodiversity, soil erosion, and the degradation of water and air quality. The destruction of natural habitats has also led to the loss of species, which can disrupt ecosystems and lead to a decline in ecosystem services, such as pollination and soil fertility.

The impacts of climate change and environmental degradation are also felt on a global scale. Climate change has led to the displacement of millions of people due to rising sea levels, more frequent and severe weather events, and the degradation of agricultural lands. The loss of biodiversity and the degradation of ecosystems also have far-reaching impacts, as these systems provide a range of services that are essential to human well-being, such as water purification, nutrient cycling, and climate regulation. The economic impacts of climate change and environmental degradation are also significant, as these issues can lead to the loss of jobs and economic opportunities, as well as increased healthcare costs and insurance premiums.

Potential Solutions to Climate Change and Environmental Degradation

There are a range of potential solutions to climate change and environmental degradation, ranging from individual actions to global policy initiatives. At the individual level, people can take actions such as reducing their energy consumption, using public transportation, and eating a plant-based diet to reduce their greenhouse gas emissions. People can also take actions such as reducing their use of single-use plastics, conserving water, and supporting sustainable agriculture practices to reduce environmental degradation.

At the community level, there are a range of initiatives that can be undertaken to address climate change and environmental degradation. These initiatives can include promoting renewable energy, supporting local food systems, and implementing green infrastructure, such as green roofs and rain gardens, to reduce stormwater runoff and improve air quality. Communities can also work to restore degraded habitats and promote biodiversity conservation.

At the national and international levels, there are a range of policy initiatives that can be implemented to address climate change and environmental degradation. These policies can include regulations and incentives to promote renewable energy and energy efficiency, such as carbon pricing and renewable portfolio standards. Governments can also implement regulations to reduce greenhouse gas emissions from industry and transportation, such as fuel efficiency standards and emissions trading systems. International agreements, such as the Paris Agreement, can also play a key role in addressing climate change by promoting global cooperation and setting targets for reducing greenhouse gas emissions.

Conclusion

Climate change and environmental degradation are two of the biggest threats facing our planet, and they are interconnected issues that require urgent action. The causes and impacts of these issues are complex and far-reaching, but there are a range of potential solutions that can be implemented at the individual, community, national, and international levels. It is up to all of us to take action to address these issues, whether through individual actions or advocacy for policy change. By working together, we can ensure a more sustainable and equitable future for all.

Introduction

Income inequality and poverty are two interrelated issues that continue to plague societies worldwide. While income inequality refers to the uneven distribution of wealth and income among different individuals and groups, poverty is a state of deprivation characterized by a lack of basic necessities such as food, shelter, and clothing. Income inequality is a major cause of poverty and has numerous negative consequences, including decreased social mobility, reduced economic growth, and increased crime rates. This article will examine the causes and consequences of income inequality and poverty and explore potential solutions.

Causes of Income Inequality and Poverty

1. Globalization and Technological Advancements

The rise of globalization and technological advancements has created significant income disparities between countries, as well as within countries. The globalization of labor markets and the increased use of technology in production have led to the outsourcing of jobs and the replacement of workers with machines. This has resulted in decreased demand for low-skilled workers and increased demand for high-skilled workers, leading to widening income inequality.

2. Economic Policies

Economic policies such as tax cuts for the wealthy, deregulation, and reductions in social welfare programs can exacerbate income inequality. Such policies favor the interests of the wealthy and contribute to the concentration of wealth in the hands of a few.

3. Discrimination and Bias

Discrimination and bias on the basis of race, gender, sexual orientation, and other factors contribute to income inequality. Women, people of color, and LGBTQ+ individuals are often paid less than their white, male counterparts and face barriers to career advancement.

Consequences of Income Inequality and Poverty

1. Reduced Social Mobility

Income inequality reduces social mobility by limiting access to education and job opportunities. Children from low-income families are less likely to attend college and are more likely to experience intergenerational poverty than children from high-income families. This perpetuates income inequality and creates a cycle of poverty that is difficult to break.

2. Reduced Economic Growth

Income inequality can also reduce economic growth by reducing demand for goods and services. When the wealthy hold a disproportionate share of wealth, they tend to save more and spend less, which can reduce aggregate demand and slow economic growth.

3. Increased Crime Rates

Studies have shown that income inequality is associated with higher crime rates. This is because poverty and income inequality create conditions that increase the likelihood of criminal behavior, such as lack of access to education and job opportunities, social isolation, and desperation.

Potential Solutions to Income Inequality and Poverty

1. Progressive Taxation

One potential solution to income inequality is progressive taxation. This involves increasing taxes on the wealthy and using the revenue to fund social welfare programs such as education, healthcare, and affordable housing. Progressive taxation can help to reduce income inequality by redistributing wealth and leveling the playing field.

2. Education and Job Training

Education and job training programs can help to reduce income inequality by providing individuals with the skills and knowledge necessary to secure well-paying jobs. These programs can be targeted towards low-income individuals and communities to ensure that everyone has access to the resources they need to succeed.

3. Universal Basic Income

Universal basic income (UBI) is a policy proposal that involves giving every citizen a guaranteed minimum income regardless of their employment status. UBI has the potential to reduce poverty and income inequality by providing a safety net for those who are unable to find work or who are underemployed.

Workplace policies such as equal pay for equal work, paid parental leave, and flexible work arrangements can help to reduce income inequality by ensuring that all workers have access to the same opportunities and benefits. These policies can also help to address discrimination and bias in the workplace.

Conclusion

Income inequality and poverty are complex issues that require a multifaceted approach to address. By implementing policies such as progressive taxation, education and job training programs, universal basic income, and workplace policies, we can begin to reduce income inequality and alleviate poverty. It is important to recognize that income inequality and poverty have negative consequences not only for those directly affected but for society as a whole. Addressing these issues is essential for creating a more just and equitable society. It is also important to acknowledge that these solutions require political will and collective action. We must work together to create a society that values and prioritizes the well-being of all its members.

Introduction

Access to quality education and healthcare are two crucial factors in determining an individual's overall wellbeing and success. Education helps individuals acquire knowledge, skills, and values necessary to lead productive lives, while healthcare ensures that people are physically and mentally healthy enough to achieve their full potential. Unfortunately, not everyone has access to these fundamental resources, which can significantly limit their opportunities in life. In this article, we will explore the importance of quality education and healthcare and examine the challenges people face in accessing these resources.

The Importance of Quality Education

Education is critical to the growth and development of individuals, communities, and nations. Quality education equips individuals with the necessary knowledge and skills to lead productive lives and contribute to their communities. Access to education is essential for breaking the cycle of poverty and promoting economic growth.

Education also has several social benefits, including reducing gender inequality and improving social cohesion. Women with access to education are more likely to marry later, have fewer children, and have better maternal health. Educated individuals are more likely to participate in democratic processes and understand the importance of civil liberties.

In addition, education has a positive impact on health outcomes. Studies show that education levels are positively associated with better health outcomes, including lower mortality rates, reduced risk of chronic diseases, and improved mental health. Education is also associated with better health behaviors, including healthy eating habits, regular exercise, and reduced risk-taking behaviors.

The Importance of Quality Healthcare

Healthcare is a fundamental human right, and access to quality healthcare is crucial for achieving good health outcomes. Healthcare encompasses a wide range of services, including preventive care, diagnostic services, and treatment for acute and chronic illnesses. Quality healthcare ensures that individuals receive timely, effective, and safe care that meets their needs.

Access to quality healthcare has several benefits, including improving health outcomes and reducing healthcare costs. Effective healthcare services can prevent illnesses, manage chronic conditions, and reduce the need for expensive medical procedures. Access to healthcare also promotes economic growth by reducing absenteeism and increasing productivity.

Challenges in Accessing Quality Education and Healthcare

Despite the importance of quality education and healthcare, many individuals face significant barriers to accessing these resources. Some of the most significant challenges include:

1. Financial Barriers: Financial barriers are one of the most significant obstacles to accessing quality education and healthcare. Many individuals cannot afford the high cost of education or healthcare services, particularly in low-income countries. Lack of financial resources often results in individuals choosing between paying for essential needs, such as food and housing, and accessing healthcare or education.

2. Geographic Barriers: Geographic barriers, including distance and lack of transportation, can significantly limit access to quality education and healthcare. Individuals living in rural or remote areas often face challenges accessing healthcare services, particularly specialized care. Similarly, students living in remote areas may not have access to quality education, particularly in subjects such as science and technology.

3. Cultural and Social Barriers: Cultural and social barriers, including gender inequality and discrimination, can limit access to education and healthcare for some individuals. Women and girls, in particular, often face significant challenges accessing education and healthcare due to cultural and social norms that prioritize male education and health.

4. Health System Challenges: Health system challenges, including limited healthcare resources and inadequate healthcare infrastructure, can limit access to quality healthcare. Many low-income countries struggle to provide basic healthcare services, including immunizations and primary care services, due to limited resources and infrastructure.

5. Educational System Challenges: Educational system challenges, including limited resources and inadequate

infrastructure, can limit access to quality education. Many low-income countries struggle to provide basic education services, including adequate facilities and qualified teachers, due to limited resources.

Strategies for Improving Access to Quality Education and Healthcare

Improving access to quality education and healthcare requires a multifaceted approach that addresses the underlying causes of these challenges. Some strategies for improving access to quality education and healthcare include:

1. Financial Support: Governments and international organizations can provide financial support to individuals and communities to improve access to education and healthcare. For example, scholarships, grants, and subsidies can help low-income families access education and healthcare services.

2. Infrastructure and Resources: Investing in infrastructure and resources, such as healthcare facilities, medical equipment, and educational facilities, can improve access to quality healthcare and education services. Governments and international organizations can provide funding and technical assistance to support infrastructure development.

3. Technology: Technology can help overcome geographic barriers to education and healthcare. Telemedicine, for example, enables healthcare providers to deliver services remotely, while online learning platforms can provide access to education resources to individuals in remote or underserved areas.

4. Community-Based Programs: Community-based programs that engage local communities can improve access to education and healthcare services. Programs that provide healthcare services in remote areas or educational programs in rural communities can help overcome geographic and social barriers.

5. Addressing Cultural and Social Norms: Addressing cultural and social norms that limit access to education and healthcare services can improve access for underserved populations. For example, programs that empower women and girls can help overcome gender inequality, while education programs that incorporate local languages and cultures can improve access for minority populations.

6. Collaboration and Partnership: Collaboration and partnership between governments, international organizations, and civil society organizations can help address systemic challenges and improve access to education and healthcare services. Collaborative efforts can lead to more effective and sustainable solutions that benefit underserved communities.

Conclusion

Access to quality education and healthcare is critical for promoting individual and community development and improving health outcomes. However, many individuals face significant barriers to accessing these resources, including financial, geographic, cultural and social, and systemic challenges. Improving access to education and healthcare requires a multifaceted approach that addresses the underlying causes of these challenges. Strategies such as financial support, infrastructure and resources, technology, community-based programs, addressing cultural and social norms, and collaboration and partnership can help overcome these barriers and improve access to quality education and healthcare services. By working together, governments, international organizations, and civil society can help ensure that all individuals have access to the resources they need to achieve their full potential and lead healthy, productive lives.

Chapter 4. Political polarization and division

Introduction

In recent years, political polarization and division have become increasingly prevalent issues in many countries around the world. People are becoming more and more divided along political lines, with each side holding on to their beliefs and refusing to compromise or even listen to the other side. This has led to a breakdown in communication, an increase in hostility, and a lack of progress on important issues. In this article, we will explore the causes and consequences of political polarization and division, as well as possible solutions to this problem.

Causes of Political Polarization and Division

1. Social Media

Social media has played a significant role in fueling political polarization and division. Platforms like Facebook and Twitter have made it easy for people to connect with others who share their beliefs and opinions, forming echo chambers where individuals are only exposed to ideas and opinions that reinforce their own. This has led to a lack of exposure to opposing viewpoints and a decreased ability to empathize with those who hold different beliefs.

2. Partisan Media

Another contributing factor to political polarization and division is the rise of partisan media. Cable news networks and websites cater to specific political ideologies, creating a media environment where individuals are only exposed to news and information that supports their beliefs. This has led to a lack of trust in mainstream media sources and a decrease in the ability to have productive conversations across political divides.

3. Identity Politics

Identity politics has become increasingly prevalent in recent years, with individuals identifying strongly with their race, gender, religion, or other personal characteristics. This has led to a situation where political disagreements are often framed as attacks on one's identity, leading to a defensive and entrenched mindset that makes compromise difficult.

Consequences of Political Polarization and Division

1. Decreased Trust

Political polarization and division have led to a decreased trust in institutions, including government, media, and even science. This lack of trust has serious consequences, making it difficult to achieve progress on important issues and leading to a breakdown in democratic processes.

2. Hostility and Anger

Political polarization and division have also led to an increase in hostility and anger between individuals and groups with different beliefs. This can lead to a lack of empathy and understanding, making it difficult to work together to solve problems.

3. Gridlock and Stagnation

Finally, political polarization and division have led to gridlock and stagnation in government, making it difficult to achieve progress on important issues. This can lead to a lack of faith in the political system and a sense of disillusionment among voters.

Possible Solutions to Political Polarization and Division

1. Encourage Media Literacy

One solution to political polarization and division is to encourage media literacy among the general population. This includes teaching individuals how to critically evaluate media sources and recognize bias, as well as promoting the consumption of a diverse range of news and information.

2. Foster Empathy and Understanding

Another solution is to foster empathy and understanding between individuals and groups with different beliefs. This can be achieved through dialogue and engagement across political divides, as well as through the promotion of education and exposure to diverse perspectives.

3. Promote Compromise and Cooperation

Finally, promoting compromise and cooperation between individuals and groups with different beliefs is essential to addressing political polarization and division. This can be achieved through the promotion of collaborative problem-solving and the de-emphasis of partisan politics.

Conclusion

Political polarization and division are serious issues that have significant consequences for society as a whole. However, by understanding the causes of polarization and division and working to promote media literacy, empathy and understanding, and compromise and cooperation, we can begin to address these problems and work towards a more united and productive society.

Introduction

Discrimination and prejudice based on race, gender, religion, and sexual orientation are social issues that have been around for centuries. They are often the result of deeply ingrained biases that affect how people view and treat individuals who are different from themselves. These biases can manifest in various ways, from subtle microaggressions to outright acts of hate and violence. In this article, we will explore the causes and effects of discrimination and prejudice based on these four characteristics, and what can be done to combat them.

Race

Race-based discrimination and prejudice are the result of centuries of systemic racism that have created significant disparities in opportunities and outcomes for people of color. This has been perpetuated through policies and practices that explicitly or implicitly favor white people and exclude people of color. For example, redlining practices in the mid-20th century denied black people access to housing and loans, which contributed to the wealth gap between white and black families. Similarly, discriminatory hiring practices and the underfunding of schools in communities of color have contributed to lower rates of employment and educational attainment for people of color.

The effects of race-based discrimination and prejudice are widespread and long-lasting. Individuals who experience discrimination based on their race may feel isolated and unsupported, and may struggle to achieve their goals. They may also experience stress and trauma as a result of the discrimination, which can have negative health effects. Moreover, systemic discrimination based on race contributes to economic and social inequality, which has ripple effects throughout society.

Gender

Gender-based discrimination and prejudice are the result of deeply ingrained beliefs about the roles and capabilities of men and women. This can manifest in various ways, from subtle biases in hiring and promotion decisions to sexual harassment and assault. Women are often paid less than men for the same work, and are underrepresented in positions of power and influence. Similarly, transgender individuals may face discrimination based on their gender identity, including being denied access to healthcare and experiencing harassment and violence.

The effects of gender-based discrimination and prejudice can be severe. Women who experience discrimination may feel undervalued and unsupported, and may struggle to achieve their career goals. They may also experience harassment and violence, which can have long-lasting mental and physical health effects. Moreover, systemic discrimination based on gender contributes to economic and social inequality, which affects not only women but also their families and communities.

Religion

Religious discrimination and prejudice are based on biases against people who belong to different religious groups. This can manifest in various ways, from verbal harassment and exclusion to acts of violence and terrorism. Muslims, in particular, have been the targets of discrimination and prejudice since the terrorist attacks of September 11, 2001. This has contributed to the stigmatization of Muslims and has led to policies such as the travel ban, which restricts travel from predominantly Muslim countries.

The effects of religious discrimination and prejudice can be devastating. Individuals who are discriminated against based on their religion may feel marginalized and ostracized from their communities. They may also experience fear and anxiety about their safety, which can affect their mental and physical health. Moreover, systemic discrimination based on religion can contribute to social and economic inequality, which can have long-term consequences for individuals and communities.

Sexual Orientation

Discrimination and prejudice based on sexual orientation are based on biases against people who identify as lesbian, gay, bisexual, or transgender (LGBT). This can manifest in various ways, from exclusion and harassment to violence and hate crimes. LGBT individuals may face discrimination in employment, housing, and healthcare, and may experience verbal and physical harassment in public spaces.

The effects of discrimination and prejudice based on sexual orientation can be severe. Individuals who are discriminated against based on their sexual orientation may feel isolated and unsupported, and may struggle to achieve their personal and professional goals. They may also experience stress and trauma as a result of the discrimination, which can have negative mental and physical health effects. Moreover, systemic discrimination based on sexual orientation can contribute to social and economic inequality, which can have long-term consequences for individuals and communities.

Combating Discrimination and Prejudice

To combat discrimination and prejudice based on race, gender, religion, and sexual orientation, individuals and society as a whole must take action. This includes recognizing and confronting biases, advocating for policy changes, and creating inclusive environments where everyone feels valued and supported.

One way to combat discrimination and prejudice is through education and awareness-raising. This includes providing education about the historical and systemic roots of discrimination, as well as training on how to recognize and combat biases. In addition, it is essential to create safe spaces where individuals can share their experiences and perspectives, and to listen to and amplify marginalized voices.

Another way to combat discrimination and prejudice is through policy changes. This includes implementing anti-discrimination laws and regulations, as well as promoting diversity and inclusion in all areas of society. For example, policies that promote diversity in hiring and promotion decisions can help combat gender-based discrimination, while policies that prohibit discrimination based on religion can help combat religious discrimination.

Finally, creating inclusive environments where everyone feels valued and supported is essential to combatting discrimination and prejudice. This includes creating workplaces and communities that celebrate diversity and actively work to address biases and discrimination. It also includes promoting empathy and understanding among individuals, and creating opportunities for dialogue and mutual respect.

Conclusion

Discrimination and prejudice based on race, gender, religion, and sexual orientation are significant social issues that have long-lasting and far-reaching consequences. They are the result of deeply ingrained biases that affect how people view and treat individuals who are different from themselves. To combat discrimination and prejudice, individuals and society as a whole must take action. This includes recognizing and confronting biases, advocating for policy changes, and creating inclusive environments where everyone feels valued and supported. By working together, we can create a more just and equitable society where everyone has the opportunity to thrive.

Introduction

As technology advances and more of our daily lives are conducted online, cybersecurity and privacy concerns have become more prevalent. Cybersecurity refers to the protection of computer systems and networks from theft, damage, or unauthorized access. Privacy, on the other hand, is the ability to keep personal information and activities private and out of the hands of unauthorized individuals or entities. In this article, we will explore the various cybersecurity and privacy concerns that people face in today's digital age.

Cybersecurity threats

Cybersecurity threats come in many forms, including viruses, malware, and phishing scams. Viruses are malicious programs that infect computer systems and can spread to other computers through the internet, email attachments, or other means. Malware refers to any type of software that is designed to harm computer systems or networks, such as spyware, ransomware, and trojans. Phishing scams involve tricking individuals into giving up their personal information, such as passwords or credit card numbers, through fake websites or emails that appear to be from legitimate sources.

Another cybersecurity threat is hacking, which involves gaining unauthorized access to computer systems or networks. Hackers can steal sensitive information, such as financial data, personal information, or intellectual property. Cyberattacks on businesses can also cause significant financial damage through theft of intellectual property or financial information, loss of customer trust, and damage to reputation.

Privacy concerns

Privacy concerns arise when personal information is collected, stored, or used without consent. In today's digital age, individuals share vast amounts of personal information online, from social media profiles to online shopping habits. Companies collect this information for a variety of purposes, such as targeted advertising, market research, or improving their products and services.

However, the collection and use of personal information can also pose significant privacy risks. Data breaches can result in sensitive information being exposed, such as credit card numbers, social security numbers, or health information. Companies may also sell or share personal information with third parties without individuals' knowledge or consent, which can lead to targeted advertising, identity theft, or other forms of exploitation.

Privacy concerns also arise in relation to government surveillance. In many countries, governments have the legal authority to monitor electronic communications and collect data on citizens for national security purposes. However, this can lead to violations of civil liberties and the right to privacy, especially if the government oversteps its legal authority or uses the information for purposes other than national security.

Protecting cybersecurity and privacy

There are several steps individuals and organizations can take to protect themselves against cybersecurity and privacy threats. One important step is to use strong passwords and two-factor authentication to protect online accounts. Individuals should also be cautious about clicking on links or downloading attachments from unknown sources, as these can contain viruses or malware.

Organizations can take steps to protect their networks, such as implementing firewalls, encrypting data, and conducting regular security audits. Businesses should also train employees on how to identify and avoid phishing scams and other types of cyberattacks.

Individuals can also take steps to protect their privacy online. This includes using privacy settings on social media platforms to control who can see their information, avoiding sharing personal information with unknown individuals or websites, and being cautious about giving out personal information online.

Organizations can also take steps to protect individuals' privacy by being transparent about their data collection practices, providing individuals with the ability to opt-out of data collection, and ensuring that personal information is stored securely and only accessed by authorized individuals.

Government regulations

Governments around the world are increasingly recognizing the importance of cybersecurity and privacy, and many have implemented regulations to protect individuals and organizations. In the United States, for example, the General Data Protection Regulation (GDPR) requires companies to obtain explicit consent before collecting personal data and to provide individuals with the ability to access, correct, or delete their data. Other countries, such as Canada and the European Union, have also implemented similar regulations to protect privacy.

In addition, many governments have established cybersecurity frameworks and guidelines to help organizations improve their cybersecurity posture. For example, the National Institute of Standards and Technology (NIST) in the United States has developed a cybersecurity framework that provides guidance on best practices for managing cybersecurity risk.

However, government regulations can also be controversial, as they may be seen as infringing on individuals' rights to privacy and freedom of speech. It is important for governments to strike a balance between protecting cybersecurity and privacy and respecting individuals' rights.

Conclusion

Cybersecurity and privacy concerns are becoming increasingly important in today's digital age. Cybersecurity threats such as viruses, malware, and hacking can cause significant financial and reputational damage, while privacy concerns arise when personal information is collected and used without consent. To protect against these threats, individuals and organizations should take steps to improve their cybersecurity and privacy practices. Governments can also play a role by implementing regulations and providing guidance on best practices for managing cybersecurity risk. Ultimately, it is important for individuals, organizations, and governments to work together to protect cybersecurity and privacy in today's digital world.

Introduction

In today's world, debt has become an increasingly common aspect of our lives. From student loans to credit card debt, mortgages, and car loans, many of us carry some form of debt. While taking on debt is often necessary to achieve certain goals or to deal with unexpected expenses, the rising levels of debt can also lead to financial instability, especially when we cannot manage it effectively. In this article, we will discuss the increasing levels of debt and financial instability, their causes, and potential solutions.

What is debt and financial instability?

Debt is the amount of money that we owe to others, whether it be to financial institutions, friends, or family members. Financial instability is a condition where an individual or a country cannot meet their financial obligations due to various factors such as high debt levels, economic downturns, or unexpected expenses. In simpler terms, it is a situation where we are unable to pay off our debts, leading to financial stress and uncertainty.

Causes of increasing levels of debt

There are several reasons why debt levels are increasing worldwide. Below are some of the primary reasons:

1. Low-interest rates: Central banks around the world have been keeping interest rates low to stimulate economic growth. While this has helped to spur borrowing and

spending, it has also encouraged people to take on more debt, as the cost of borrowing is lower.

2. Easy credit: Financial institutions have made it easier for people to access credit in recent years. Lenders are more willing to lend to people with lower credit scores, and the process of applying for credit has become quicker and more streamlined. This has led to more people taking on debt, which can be a problem when they cannot repay it.

3. High living costs: The cost of living has risen dramatically in recent years, making it harder for people to make ends meet. As a result, many people turn to credit to help them pay for essential expenses such as housing, food, and transportation.

4. Unemployment and underemployment: High levels of unemployment and underemployment can make it difficult for people to pay off their debts. If someone loses their job, they may be unable to make their monthly payments, which can lead to financial instability.

5. Medical expenses: Healthcare costs have skyrocketed in recent years, and many people are unable to afford medical bills. As a result, they may turn to credit to pay for medical expenses, which can add to their overall debt load.

Consequences of financial instability

Financial instability can have severe consequences for individuals and the economy. Some of the significant effects of financial instability are:

1. Bankruptcy: If individuals or businesses cannot pay off their debts, they may file for bankruptcy, which can have a significant impact on their credit score and financial future.

2. Reduced access to credit: Financial instability can make it harder for individuals to access credit in the future, as lenders may view them as high-risk borrowers.

3. Stress and anxiety: High levels of debt can lead to stress and anxiety, which can impact an individual's mental and physical health.

4. Impact on the economy: High levels of debt can lead to economic instability, as seen during the 2008 financial crisis. When people cannot pay off their debts, it can lead to a domino effect, impacting banks, financial institutions, and the broader economy.

Solutions to reduce financial instability

There are several potential solutions to reduce financial instability and address the rising levels of debt. Below are some of the ways that individuals, governments, and financial institutions can take action.

1. Education: Education is key to reducing financial instability. Individuals need to understand the consequences of taking on debt and learn how to manage their finances effectively. Governments can provide financial education programs to help individuals better understand their finances and make informed decisions.

2. Debt restructuring: Debt restructuring is a process where an individual or business works with creditors to negotiate a new payment plan that is more manageable. This can include reducing the interest rate, extending the payment term, or reducing the total amount owed. Debt restructuring can help individuals and businesses avoid bankruptcy and reduce financial stress.

3. Debt consolidation: Debt consolidation is another strategy to reduce debt levels. This involves combining multiple debts into one loan, which can have a lower interest rate and more manageable payment terms. Debt consolidation can help individuals pay off their debts more quickly and reduce their overall debt load.

4. Increased regulation: Governments can implement policies and regulations to reduce financial instability. For example, they can introduce stricter lending requirements for financial institutions to reduce the number of high-risk borrowers. They can also limit the amount of debt that individuals can take on to prevent them from becoming overwhelmed with debt.

5. Improve economic conditions: A robust economy with low levels of unemployment and strong economic growth can help reduce financial instability. Governments can implement policies to stimulate economic growth, such as investing in infrastructure or providing tax incentives to businesses.

6. Work with financial advisors: Working with a financial advisor can help individuals develop a comprehensive financial plan that includes debt management. A financial advisor can provide guidance on budgeting, debt repayment strategies, and investment options that can help individuals reduce their debt load and achieve their financial goals.

Conclusion

Rising levels of debt are a significant concern, as it can lead to financial instability for individuals, businesses, and countries. Understanding the causes of increasing levels of debt and the consequences of financial instability is critical to addressing this issue. Solutions such as education, debt restructuring, debt consolidation, increased regulation, improving economic conditions, and working with financial advisors can help individuals and governments reduce financial instability and create a more stable financial future. Ultimately, it is up to individuals to take control of their finances and manage their debt effectively to avoid financial stress and uncertainty.

Chapter 8. Displacement of people due to war, conflict, and natural disasters

Introduction

The displacement of people due to war, conflict, and natural disasters is a global problem that affects millions of individuals every year. It is a phenomenon that has been ongoing for centuries, and despite efforts to address it, it remains a persistent issue. Displacement refers to the forced movement of individuals from their homes, often to other parts of their own country or even abroad, due to various reasons.

This article will delve deeper into the various causes of displacement and their effects on individuals and society. We will also examine the measures that are in place to support displaced individuals and communities.

Causes of displacement

There are three main causes of displacement: war, conflict, and natural disasters. These three factors often overlap, and their combined effects can exacerbate the displacement crisis.

1. War and conflict

Wars and conflicts have been a significant cause of displacement throughout history. These events can lead to the destruction of homes and communities, as well as the loss of life and livelihoods. The Syrian conflict, for example, has resulted in the displacement of over 13 million people since 2011.

In many cases, war and conflict are fueled by political, religious, or ethnic tensions. These tensions can lead to the persecution of certain groups, further exacerbating the displacement crisis. The Rohingya refugee crisis in Myanmar is an example of this, with over one million people forced to flee the country due to persecution and violence.

2. Natural disasters

Natural disasters such as hurricanes, floods, earthquakes, and wildfires can also lead to displacement. These events can cause significant damage to infrastructure and homes, making them uninhabitable. In some cases, natural disasters can also lead to the loss of life and livelihoods.

Climate change is also contributing to the displacement crisis, as extreme weather events become more frequent and severe. The World Bank estimates that by 2050, 143 million people could be displaced due to the impacts of climate change.

3. Combination of factors

In many cases, displacement is caused by a combination of factors. For example, conflict in Syria has been exacerbated by a severe drought that has led to food shortages and economic hardship.

Effects of displacement

The effects of displacement can be long-lasting and profound. Displaced individuals often face a range of challenges, including:

1. Loss of livelihoods

Displacement can lead to the loss of homes, businesses, and other assets, making it difficult for individuals to make a living. This can lead to poverty and economic insecurity, further exacerbating the displacement crisis.

2. Health risks

Displaced individuals often face significant health risks, including malnutrition, exposure to the elements, and the spread of diseases such as cholera and COVID-19. Access to healthcare can also be limited, particularly in areas affected by conflict or natural disasters.

3. Psychological trauma

Displacement can be traumatic, particularly for children who may be separated from their families or exposed to violence and other forms of trauma. The psychological effects of displacement can be long-lasting, affecting mental health and well-being.

4. Social disruption

Displacement can disrupt social networks and communities, leading to a breakdown of social support systems. This can further exacerbate the psychological effects of displacement, as individuals may feel isolated and disconnected from their communities.

5. Education disruption

Displacement can disrupt education, with many children forced to drop out of school due to the loss of their homes or the need to work to support their families. This can lead to a generation of children who lack access to education, further exacerbating poverty and economic insecurity.

Support for displaced individuals

Governments, international organizations, and NGOs play a vital role in supporting displaced individuals and communities. There are several key measures in place to support displaced individuals:

1. Emergency aid

Emergency aid such as food, water, and shelter is provided to displaced individuals in the immediate aftermath of a crisis. This can help to address the immediate needs of those affected and prevent further harm.

2. Refugee and asylum programs

Refugee and asylum programs are in place to provide a safe haven for individuals who have been forced to flee their homes. These programs provide protection and support for those who are at risk of persecution or harm.

3. Long-term support

Long-term support programs are essential for displaced individuals to rebuild their lives and communities. This can include education and training programs, economic support, and access to healthcare and other essential services.

4. International cooperation

International cooperation is crucial to addressing the displacement crisis. Governments, NGOs, and international organizations must work together to provide coordinated and effective responses to displacement crises.

Challenges and solutions

Despite efforts to address the displacement crisis, there are several challenges that need to be addressed. These include:

1. Funding

The funding required to address the displacement crisis is significant, and there is often a lack of financial support for long-term programs. Governments and international organizations must prioritize funding for displacement programs to ensure that those affected receive the support they need.

2. Legal barriers

Legal barriers can prevent displaced individuals from accessing essential services and support. This can include restrictions on movement, employment, and access to education and healthcare. Governments and international organizations must work together to address these barriers and ensure that displaced individuals have access to the support they need.

3. Discrimination and stigma

Displaced individuals may face discrimination and stigma from the communities they are displaced to, making it difficult for them to rebuild their lives. This can lead to social isolation and further exacerbate the psychological effects of displacement. Governments and international organizations must work to address discrimination and stigma and promote social inclusion for displaced individuals.

4. Capacity building

Governments and international organizations must build capacity to address the displacement crisis effectively. This includes building the capacity of local organizations and communities to provide support to those affected by displacement.

Conclusion

The displacement of people due to war, conflict, and natural disasters is a global problem that affects millions of individuals every year. Displacement can have long-lasting and profound effects on individuals and society. Governments, international organizations, and NGOs play a vital role in providing support to displaced individuals and communities.

There are several key measures in place to address the displacement crisis, including emergency aid, refugee and asylum programs, and long-term support programs. However, there are several challenges that need to be addressed, including funding, legal barriers, discrimination and stigma, and capacity building.

Addressing the displacement crisis requires coordinated and effective responses from governments, international organizations, and NGOs. By working together, we can provide the support and protection that displaced individuals need to rebuild their lives and communities.

Chapter 9. Global pandemic and public health crises

Introduction

The world has faced many public health crises, but none have been as far-reaching and widespread as the global COVID-19 pandemic. The pandemic has affected every aspect of human life, from health and wellbeing to social and economic stability. The crisis has brought to the fore the importance of public health and the need for a global response to pandemics. This article explores the impact of the COVID-19 pandemic on public health, the global response to the crisis, and what can be done to prevent future pandemics.

The Impact of the Pandemic on Public Health

The COVID-19 pandemic has had a profound impact on public health worldwide. The virus has infected millions of people and claimed the lives of hundreds of thousands. The pandemic has also affected mental health, with many people experiencing anxiety, depression, and other psychological effects. The pandemic has highlighted the importance of public health infrastructure and the need for effective public health policies to respond to outbreaks.

The pandemic has also exposed the inequalities in global health. People in low-income countries are more vulnerable to the virus due to inadequate healthcare systems, poverty, and limited access to clean water and sanitation. The pandemic has also had a disproportionate impact on marginalized communities, such as people of color and those living in poverty. These communities are more likely to have pre-existing health conditions, which can make them more vulnerable to the virus.

Global Response to the Pandemic

The global response to the pandemic has been mixed. While some countries have been successful in containing the virus, others have struggled to control its spread. The World Health Organization (WHO) has played a key role in coordinating the global response to the pandemic. The organization has provided guidance on how to prevent the spread of the virus, tested and treated patients, and developed vaccines.

The development of vaccines has been a critical component of the global response to the pandemic. Several vaccines have been developed and approved for use, with millions of doses administered worldwide. The vaccines have been effective in reducing the spread of the virus and preventing severe illness and death. However, there have been challenges in distributing the vaccines equitably, with wealthy countries obtaining most of the doses while poorer countries struggle to access them.

Preventing Future Pandemics

Preventing future pandemics requires a coordinated global response. The WHO has outlined several strategies for preventing pandemics, including early detection, rapid response, and improving public health infrastructure. Early detection of outbreaks is critical to preventing their spread, and countries must invest in surveillance systems to detect potential outbreaks quickly.

Rapid response is also essential to prevent the spread of pandemics. Countries must have the capacity to respond quickly to outbreaks, including deploying healthcare workers, providing medical supplies and equipment, and implementing measures to control the spread of the virus. Investing in public health infrastructure is also critical to preventing future pandemics. This includes strengthening healthcare systems, improving sanitation and hygiene, and ensuring access to clean water.

Conclusion

The COVID-19 pandemic has highlighted the importance of public health and the need for a coordinated global response to pandemics. The pandemic has had a profound impact on public health worldwide, highlighting the inequalities in global health and the need for effective public health policies to respond to outbreaks. The global response to the pandemic has been mixed, with some countries successfully containing the virus while others struggle to control its spread. Preventing future pandemics requires a coordinated global response, including early detection, rapid response, and investment in public health infrastructure. By working together, we can prevent future pandemics and ensure the health and wellbeing of people worldwide.

Introduction

Nuclear weapons proliferation is a serious global concern. The threat of war and the use of nuclear weapons have been inextricably linked since their inception. The spread of nuclear weapons to additional states increases the likelihood of a catastrophic conflict. The risk of accidental or intentional nuclear war is heightened by the existence of multiple nuclear-armed states, each with their own military doctrines and strategic postures. In this article, we will explore the issues surrounding nuclear weapons proliferation and the potential for war.

The history of nuclear proliferation

The history of nuclear proliferation begins with the United States and its development of the atomic bomb during World War II. The US used the bomb on Japan in August 1945, killing over 100,000 people and causing immense devastation. The Soviet Union became the second nuclear power in 1949, and the UK, France, and China followed in the subsequent decades. These five states became the only recognized nuclear-armed states under the Non-Proliferation Treaty (NPT), signed in 1968. Since then, several other states have developed nuclear weapons, including India, Pakistan, and North Korea. Israel is also widely believed to possess nuclear weapons, although it has never officially acknowledged this.

The dangers of nuclear weapons proliferation

The spread of nuclear weapons to additional states poses significant dangers. First, it increases the likelihood of a nuclear war. The more states that possess nuclear weapons, the greater the potential for accidents or misunderstandings that could lead to a catastrophic conflict. Second, it creates a destabilizing effect in regions where multiple states possess nuclear weapons. The possibility of a nuclear exchange between India and Pakistan or between North Korea and the United States poses a significant threat to global security. Third, it undermines the NPT, which is the cornerstone of global efforts to prevent the spread of nuclear weapons. If more states acquire nuclear weapons, it could lead to a breakdown of the treaty and a return to the era of nuclear brinksmanship that characterized the Cold War.

The challenges of preventing nuclear proliferation

Preventing nuclear proliferation is a challenging task. The NPT provides a framework for preventing the spread of nuclear weapons, but it has not been entirely successful. States that have acquired nuclear weapons have done so despite the treaty's provisions. For example, North Korea withdrew from the NPT in 2003 and conducted its first nuclear test in 2006. Iran's nuclear program has been a subject of international concern for decades, and it remains a contentious issue today.

The challenges of preventing nuclear proliferation are multifaceted. First, some states view nuclear weapons as essential for their security. For example, North Korea sees nuclear weapons as a deterrent against a potential US attack. Second, some states may seek nuclear weapons for prestige or to counterbalance their neighbors' nuclear capabilities. Third, some states may seek nuclear weapons to compensate for their conventional military weaknesses. Finally, some states may seek nuclear weapons to counter a perceived threat from another nuclear-armed state.

The potential for accidental nuclear war

The existence of multiple nuclear-armed states increases the potential for accidental nuclear war. The risk of an accidental nuclear exchange is heightened by the fact that nuclear weapons are on high alert, ready to be launched at a moment's notice. This is known as the doctrine of mutually assured destruction (MAD). The theory behind MAD is that if both sides have the ability to destroy the other, neither will launch a first strike. However, the risk of an accidental launch or a misunderstanding that could trigger a nuclear exchange is significant.

The potential for intentional nuclear war

The potential for intentional nuclear war also exists. States with nuclear weapons may use them to achieve their political objectives. For example, North Korea has threatened to use nuclear weapons against the United States and its allies. In a crisis, a state may perceive the use of nuclear weapons as necessary to protect its interests or to prevent an adversary from achieving its objectives. The consequences of a nuclear war would be catastrophic, with millions of people killed and entire cities destroyed. The global economy and political landscape would be severely disrupted, and the long-term effects on human health and the environment would be incalculable.

The need for disarmament

Given the dangers posed by nuclear weapons, there is a pressing need for disarmament. The elimination of nuclear weapons would remove the risk of accidental or intentional nuclear war, and it would reduce the likelihood of proliferation. However, achieving disarmament is a daunting task. States that possess nuclear weapons are unlikely to give them up voluntarily, given the perceived strategic advantages they provide. Furthermore, the technical expertise required to produce nuclear weapons is widely available, making it difficult to prevent proliferation.

The role of international organizations

International organizations have a vital role to play in preventing nuclear proliferation and promoting disarmament. The International Atomic Energy Agency (IAEA) is responsible for verifying states' compliance with the NPT and ensuring that nuclear technology is used only for peaceful purposes. The United Nations (UN) Security Council has the authority to impose sanctions and take other measures against states that violate international norms regarding nuclear weapons. Non-governmental organizations (NGOs) also play an important role in raising awareness about the dangers of nuclear weapons and promoting disarmament.

Conclusion

Nuclear weapons proliferation poses a significant threat to global security. The risk of accidental or intentional nuclear war is heightened by the existence of multiple nuclear-armed states, each with its own military doctrines and strategic postures. Preventing nuclear proliferation is a challenging task, given the multifaceted reasons why states may seek nuclear weapons. Disarmament is the ultimate solution to the dangers posed by nuclear weapons, but achieving it is a daunting task. International organizations have a vital role to play in promoting disarmament and preventing nuclear proliferation. The dangers of nuclear weapons are too great to ignore, and the international community must work together to prevent their spread and ultimately eliminate them.

Introduction

Corruption and lack of transparency are two interrelated problems that affect both governments and corporations. Corruption is the abuse of power for personal gain, while lack of transparency refers to the absence of clear and accessible information. Together, they erode trust in institutions, undermine democracy, and impede economic growth. In this article, we will explore the causes and consequences of corruption and lack of transparency, as well as potential solutions.

Causes of Corruption and Lack of Transparency

Corruption and lack of transparency have multiple causes, including:

1. Power asymmetry: When some individuals or organizations have more power than others, they can use that power to benefit themselves and their allies. For example, politicians might receive bribes from corporations in exchange for favorable policies.

2. Weak institutions: When institutions such as courts, law enforcement agencies, and regulatory bodies are weak or ineffective, they are less able to prevent or punish corrupt behavior.

3. Lack of accountability: When there are no consequences for corrupt behavior, individuals and organizations are

more likely to engage in it. This can happen when laws are not enforced, or when those in power are able to shield themselves from scrutiny.

4. Culture of impunity: When corruption is accepted as a normal part of doing business, it can become difficult to change. This can happen when there is a history of corruption in a particular industry or country, or when those in power believe they are above the law.

Consequences of Corruption and Lack of Transparency

Corruption and lack of transparency have a wide range of negative consequences, including:

1. Economic harm: Corruption can lead to the misallocation of resources, as decisions are made based on personal gain rather than the public interest. This can lead to reduced economic growth and increased poverty.

2. Undermining democracy: When institutions are not transparent or accountable, citizens are less able to hold their leaders to account. This can erode trust in democratic processes and lead to a loss of faith in government.

3. Social harm: Corruption can perpetuate inequality, as those with more resources are better able to access corrupt networks. This can lead to social unrest and increased crime.

4. Environmental harm: Lack of transparency can make it difficult to monitor and regulate environmental impacts. This can lead to environmental damage and health risks for communities.

Potential Solutions

To address corruption and lack of transparency, a range of solutions have been proposed, including:

1. Strengthening institutions: **By** strengthening institutions such as courts, law enforcement agencies, and regulatory bodies, it becomes harder for corrupt behavior to go unpunished. This can involve providing training and resources to those working in these institutions, as well as reforming laws and regulations.

2. Promoting transparency: **By** making information more accessible, governments and corporations can increase transparency and accountability. This can involve publishing information online, creating open data portals, and providing information to citizens through public meetings and consultations.

3. Encouraging citizen engagement: **By** encouraging citizens to participate in decision-making processes, governments and corporations can increase accountability and reduce the risk of corruption. This can involve creating channels for feedback and complaints, as well as involving citizens in the design and implementation of policies.

4. Creating incentives for ethical behavior: **By** providing incentives for ethical behavior, such as rewards for whistleblowers or penalties for those engaging in corrupt behavior, governments and corporations can help create a culture that values transparency and accountability.

5. Strengthening international cooperation: **By** working together at the international level, governments and corporations can help address corruption that crosses borders. This can involve sharing information and best

practices, as well as creating international agreements and conventions.

Case Studies

To illustrate the impact of corruption and lack of transparency, we will now examine two case studies: the Watergate scandal and the 1MDB scandal.

1. Watergate Scandal

The Watergate scandal was a political scandal that took place in the United States in the 1970s. The scandal began in 1972 when five men were caught breaking into the headquarters of the Democratic National Committee at the Watergate complex in Washington, D.C. The men were later found to be connected to President Richard Nixon's re-election campaign.

As the scandal unfolded, it was revealed that the break-in was part of a broader campaign of political espionage and sabotage directed by the Nixon administration. The scandal ultimately led to the resignation of President Nixon in 1974, as well as the indictment and conviction of many of his top aides.

The Watergate scandal is a classic example of the dangers of corruption and lack of transparency in government. The Nixon administration used its power to spy on and sabotage its political opponents, and then tried to cover up its actions when they were discovered. The scandal exposed a culture of corruption and abuse of power at the highest levels of government, and demonstrated the importance of a free press and independent judiciary in holding those in power accountable.

2. 1MDB Scandal

The 1MDB scandal is a more recent example of corruption and lack of transparency, this time in the corporate world. 1MDB was a state-owned investment fund established by the Malaysian government in 2009 with the aim of promoting economic development. However, the fund quickly became embroiled in a web of corruption and mismanagement.

Over the course of several years, billions of dollars were siphoned off from the fund and used to purchase luxury properties, artwork, and other assets by a network of individuals with close ties to the Malaysian government. The scandal eventually led to the downfall of former Malaysian Prime Minister Najib Razak, who was accused of using the fund for personal gain.

The 1MDB scandal highlights the risks of corruption and lack of transparency in the corporate world. When powerful individuals and organizations are not held accountable for their actions, they can engage in corrupt behavior that harms not only shareholders but also the wider public. The scandal also highlights the importance of strong regulatory oversight and effective enforcement mechanisms to prevent and punish corrupt behavior.

Conclusion

Corruption and lack of transparency are two interrelated problems that have far-reaching consequences for society. They erode trust in institutions, undermine democracy, and impede economic growth. Addressing these problems requires a range of solutions, including strengthening institutions, promoting transparency, encouraging citizen engagement, creating incentives for ethical behavior, and strengthening international cooperation. By taking action to address corruption and lack of transparency, governments and corporations can create a more just and equitable society for all.

Introduction

Food insecurity and malnutrition are two closely related issues that are prevalent in many parts of the world. According to the World Health Organization (WHO), over 820 million people around the world do not have access to adequate food, and one in three people globally suffer from some form of malnutrition. These issues have far-reaching impacts on the health, well-being, and productivity of individuals and communities, and are major obstacles to achieving sustainable development.

What is food insecurity?

Food insecurity refers to a situation where people lack access to sufficient, safe, and nutritious food to meet their dietary needs for an active and healthy life. Food insecurity can be caused by various factors, such as poverty, climate change, conflicts, natural disasters, and inequalities in food distribution systems. The consequences of food insecurity can be severe, ranging from hunger and malnutrition to poor health outcomes and social and economic instability.

Types of food insecurity

Food insecurity can manifest in different ways and affect different populations. The following are some of the types of food insecurity:

1. Chronic food insecurity: This refers to a situation where people lack access to adequate food for prolonged periods, usually due to poverty or other structural factors.

2. Transient food insecurity: This refers to a situation where people experience food shortages due to temporary events, such as natural disasters or economic shocks.

3. Seasonal food insecurity: This refers to a situation where people experience food shortages during certain periods of the year, such as the lean season between harvests.

4. Hidden hunger: This refers to a situation where people consume enough calories but lack sufficient essential micronutrients, such as vitamins and minerals, for good health.

What is malnutrition?

Malnutrition refers to a condition where people's dietary intake is inadequate or imbalanced, resulting in negative health outcomes. Malnutrition can be caused by various factors, such as food insecurity, poor feeding practices, and underlying health conditions. The consequences of malnutrition can be severe, ranging from stunted growth and cognitive impairment to increased susceptibility to infectious diseases and premature death.

Types of malnutrition

There are three main types of malnutrition:

1. Undernutrition: This refers to a condition where people do not consume enough calories or essential nutrients to meet their dietary needs, resulting in stunted growth, wasting, and underweight.

2. Overnutrition: This refers to a condition where people consume too many calories, particularly from unhealthy foods, resulting in overweight, obesity, and related health problems, such as diabetes and cardiovascular diseases.

3. Micronutrient deficiency: This refers to a condition where people lack sufficient essential micronutrients, such as vitamins and minerals, resulting in various health problems, such as anemia, blindness, and impaired cognitive function.

The link between food insecurity and malnutrition

Food insecurity and malnutrition are closely linked, and one often leads to the other. When people do not have access to adequate food, they are more likely to experience malnutrition. Similarly, when people suffer from malnutrition, their ability to access and afford food is compromised. The consequences of food insecurity and malnutrition can be severe, particularly for vulnerable populations, such as children, pregnant women, and the elderly.

Impacts of food insecurity and malnutrition

Food insecurity and malnutrition have far-reaching impacts on individuals, communities, and societies. The following are some of the impacts of food insecurity and malnutrition:

1. Poor health outcomes: Food insecurity and malnutrition can lead to various health problems, such as stunted growth, wasting, underweight, overweight, obesity, anemia, and impaired cognitive function. These health problems can have lifelong consequences, particularly for children, and

can increase the risk of chronic diseases, such as diabetes and cardiovascular diseases.

2. Reduced productivity: Food insecurity and malnutrition can reduce people's ability to work and learn, which can have negative impacts on their productivity and economic prospects. Malnourished children, for example, may experience developmental delays that can limit their ability to learn and succeed in school, while malnourished adults may experience fatigue and reduced productivity at work.

3. Social and economic instability: Food insecurity and malnutrition can also have broader social and economic impacts. In extreme cases, food insecurity can lead to social unrest, conflict, and displacement, as people are forced to migrate in search of food and livelihoods. Similarly, malnutrition can lead to increased healthcare costs and reduced economic productivity, which can have negative impacts on national economies.

4. Inter-generational impacts: Food insecurity and malnutrition can have inter-generational impacts, particularly for women and children. Malnourished mothers, for example, are more likely to give birth to low birth weight babies, who are at increased risk of malnutrition and poor health outcomes. Similarly, malnourished children may experience developmental delays that can limit their ability to learn and succeed in school, perpetuating the cycle of poverty and food insecurity.

Addressing food insecurity and malnutrition

Addressing food insecurity and malnutrition requires a multi-faceted approach that addresses the root causes of these issues. The following are some strategies for addressing food insecurity and malnutrition:

1. Increasing access to nutritious food: Efforts to increase access to nutritious food can help address both food insecurity and malnutrition. This can include initiatives to improve food distribution systems, increase food production and availability, and promote healthier food choices.

2. Supporting vulnerable populations: Targeted interventions to support vulnerable populations, such as children, pregnant women, and the elderly, can help reduce the impacts of food insecurity and malnutrition. This can include providing nutritional supplements, promoting breastfeeding and other healthy feeding practices, and providing healthcare and other social services.

3. Addressing poverty: Addressing poverty is a key factor in reducing food insecurity and malnutrition. This can include initiatives to increase economic opportunities and reduce income inequality, as well as providing social safety nets, such as cash transfers and food assistance programs.

4. Addressing climate change: Climate change is a major driver of food insecurity and malnutrition, particularly in vulnerable communities. Addressing climate change requires global action to reduce greenhouse gas emissions and mitigate the impacts of climate change, as well as supporting adaptation strategies, such as improved water management and agricultural practices.

Conclusion

Food insecurity and malnutrition are complex issues that require a multi-faceted approach to address. The impacts of food insecurity and malnutrition are far-reaching, affecting the health, well-being, and productivity of individuals and communities. Addressing food insecurity and malnutrition requires a combination of strategies, including increasing access to nutritious food, supporting vulnerable populations, addressing poverty, and addressing climate change. By working together to address these issues, we can create a healthier, more sustainable future for all.

Introduction

As the world continues to develop and modernize, there are many demographic changes taking place. One of the most significant shifts is the aging of populations in many regions, coupled with declining birth rates. This demographic phenomenon is occurring in many developed and developing countries, including Japan, Europe, and parts of North America. This article explores the reasons behind this trend, its implications for society, and possible solutions to address the challenges posed by an aging population and declining birth rates.

Reasons behind Aging Population and Declining Birth Rates

There are several factors contributing to an aging population and declining birth rates. One major factor is the increasing age at which women are having children. Many women are delaying having children to pursue their careers, travel, and other interests. This trend has led to a decline in the number of women of childbearing age, which in turn has led to a decline in the birth rate.

Another factor is the declining fertility rate. Fertility rates have been declining for several decades, partly due to improvements in birth control methods and partly due to changes in social attitudes towards childbearing. In some countries, there are also economic factors at play, such as high living costs and difficulties in finding affordable housing. These factors can make it more challenging for families to support and raise children.

Implications of Aging Population and Declining Birth Rates

An aging population and declining birth rates have significant implications for society. One of the most significant challenges is the strain on the workforce and economy. With an aging population, there are fewer people of working age to support the elderly population, which can result in a shortage of workers and decreased productivity. In some regions, this has led to labor shortages in specific sectors, such as healthcare and social services.

Another significant challenge is the strain on healthcare and social services. As the population ages, there is an increased demand for healthcare services, such as long-term care for the elderly. There is also an increased demand for social services, such as affordable housing, transportation, and other forms of support for the elderly.

Aging populations can also result in a decline in economic growth and competitiveness. With fewer people of working age, there may be a decrease in innovation, productivity, and overall economic growth. This can result in a decline in the standard of living and overall quality of life for the population.

Solutions to Address the Challenges of an Aging Population and Declining Birth Rates

There are several solutions that policymakers can implement to address the challenges posed by an aging population and declining birth rates. One solution is to encourage immigration. Many countries with aging populations are exploring policies to attract immigrants to address labor shortages and boost economic growth. However, immigration policies can be complex, and policymakers must ensure that immigrants are integrated into society and are treated fairly.

Another solution is to provide support for families to encourage childbearing. This can include policies such as affordable childcare, paid parental leave, and tax incentives for families with children. By providing support for families, policymakers can help reduce the financial burden of raising children and make it easier for families to balance work and family responsibilities.

Governments can also invest in education and training to address labor shortages and improve productivity. By investing in education and training, policymakers can ensure that the workforce is equipped with the skills needed to compete in a global economy.

Finally, policymakers can invest in technology and innovation to improve productivity and economic growth. By investing in technology and innovation, policymakers can help address labor shortages and improve the standard of living for the population.

Conclusion

An aging population and declining birth rates are significant demographic trends that are taking place in many regions around the world. These trends have significant implications for society, including labor shortages, increased demand for healthcare and social services, and a decline in economic growth and competitiveness. However, there are several solutions that policymakers can implement to address these challenges, including encouraging immigration, providing support for families, investing in education and training, and investing in technology and innovation. These solutions will require collaboration and coordination across government, industry, and civil society to address the challenges posed by an aging population and declining birth rates.

Ultimately, addressing these challenges will require a long-term vision and commitment to change. Policymakers must work together to create policies that are sustainable and address the needs of both the young and the old. By doing so, we can create a society that is inclusive, equitable, and prosperous for all.

In conclusion, an aging population and declining birth rates are significant demographic trends that are taking place in many regions around the world. These trends have significant implications for society, including labor shortages, increased demand for healthcare and social services, and a decline in economic growth and competitiveness. However, there are several solutions that policymakers can implement to address these challenges, including encouraging immigration, providing support for families, investing in education and training, and investing in technology and innovation. By working together, we can create a more sustainable and prosperous future for all.

Chapter 14. Lack of affordable housing and rising homelessness

Introduction

Lack of affordable housing has been a significant issue worldwide, causing a surge in homelessness. The shortage of affordable housing has impacted people from all walks of life, regardless of their income level, education, or race. In recent years, the problem has worsened, with the number of homeless individuals and families rising at an alarming rate. This article explores the factors that contribute to the lack of affordable housing and the rise in homelessness.

The Housing Crisis

The shortage of affordable housing is a multifaceted problem that has been developing for decades. There are several factors that contribute to the issue. One of the main reasons is the lack of affordable housing units. In many cities, the demand for housing has surpassed the supply, which has driven up prices, making it challenging for low and middle-income earners to find affordable housing. Another factor is the increasing cost of construction and land prices. In some areas, the price of land has skyrocketed, making it difficult for developers to build affordable housing. Additionally, the rising cost of construction materials and labor has made it more expensive to build new homes, making it less likely that developers will create affordable housing.

Rising Homelessness

The shortage of affordable housing has led to a surge in homelessness. The lack of affordable housing options leaves many people with no other choice but to live on the streets or in shelters. Homelessness affects people of all ages, including families with children, veterans, and seniors. It is a devastating experience that can cause a range of health problems and other issues, including mental health concerns, drug addiction, and physical health problems.

Factors Contributing to Homelessness

Several factors contribute to homelessness. One of the leading causes is poverty. When people cannot afford housing, they may become homeless. Job loss and low wages are two common reasons people fall into poverty. Additionally, mental illness and substance abuse can also contribute to homelessness. Many homeless individuals have undiagnosed mental health conditions or drug addiction problems that make it challenging to maintain stable housing. Finally, family breakdowns and domestic violence can also lead to homelessness. When people experience family breakdowns or domestic violence, they may have nowhere else to turn but the streets.

Impact of Homelessness

Homelessness can have a profound impact on individuals, families, and communities. People who are homeless face many challenges, including lack of access to food, water, and medical care. They also face a higher risk of physical and emotional abuse. Additionally, homeless individuals are more likely to develop chronic health problems, such as respiratory illness and infectious diseases. Homelessness also affects the broader community, as it can lead to increased crime and other social problems.

Solutions to the Housing Crisis and Homelessness

To address the housing crisis and homelessness, there needs to be a comprehensive approach that includes multiple strategies. One strategy is to increase the supply of affordable housing. This can be accomplished through incentives for developers, such as tax breaks or subsidies. Governments can also use public land to build affordable housing units or provide funding to nonprofit organizations that build and manage affordable housing. Another solution is to provide rent subsidies or other forms of financial assistance to help low-income families pay for housing.

Another approach is to address the root causes of homelessness. This includes providing mental health services, substance abuse treatment, and job training programs to help individuals become self-sufficient. Programs that address domestic violence and family breakdowns can also help prevent homelessness. Finally, providing emergency shelters and other support services, such as meals and medical care, can help homeless individuals get back on their feet.

Conclusion

The lack of affordable housing and rising homelessness is a complex issue that requires a multifaceted approach. There are many factors that contribute to the problem, including the shortage of affordable housing units, rising construction and land costs, and poverty. To address the issue, there needs to be a concerted effort to increase the supply of affordable housing, provide financial assistance to low-income families, and address the root causes of homelessness. It is essential to recognize that homelessness is not an individual issue but a societal one. By investing in solutions to address homelessness, we can improve the health and well-being of individuals, families, and communities.

Furthermore, addressing the housing crisis and homelessness requires a collaborative effort between government, nonprofits, and private organizations. Each group has a role to play in providing housing and support services to those in need. Governments can enact policies that incentivize developers to build affordable housing units, while nonprofits can provide services to help individuals become self-sufficient. Private organizations can also contribute by providing funding or other resources to support affordable housing initiatives.

Finally, it is crucial to recognize that the lack of affordable housing and homelessness is a global issue. While the root causes and solutions may vary from country to country, the impact of homelessness is universal. By sharing information and best practices, we can work together to address this issue on a global scale.

In conclusion, the lack of affordable housing and rising homelessness is a significant issue that requires a comprehensive approach. There are many factors that contribute to the problem, including poverty, rising construction costs, and the shortage of affordable housing units. To address the issue, there needs to be a concerted effort to increase the supply of affordable housing, provide financial assistance to low-income families, and address the root causes of homelessness. By working together, we can make progress towards ending homelessness and ensuring that everyone has access to safe and affordable housing.

Introduction

Addiction is a complex and multifaceted disorder that affects millions of individuals across the globe. Substance use disorders, behavioral addictions, and co-occurring mental health issues are all components of addiction that require comprehensive treatment. Substance abuse and mental health issues often co-occur, and individuals who struggle with addiction frequently have underlying mental health disorders. Addiction and mental health disorders are closely intertwined, and each condition can exacerbate the symptoms of the other. Therefore, it is essential to address both the addiction and mental health issues simultaneously to achieve long-term recovery.

The Connection between Addiction and Mental Health Issues

Substance abuse and mental health issues often go hand in hand, and each condition can exacerbate the symptoms of the other. Substance abuse can lead to the development of mental health disorders, such as depression and anxiety, while individuals with pre-existing mental health disorders are more likely to abuse drugs and alcohol. The relationship between addiction and mental health issues is complex, and it is often difficult to determine which condition came first. However, research has shown that treating both conditions concurrently leads to better outcomes and higher rates of recovery.

Common Mental Health Issues Associated with Addiction

1. Depression: Individuals who struggle with addiction often experience depression, and the two conditions frequently co-occur. Depression is a mental health disorder characterized by feelings of sadness, hopelessness, and a loss of interest in activities that were once enjoyable. Substance abuse can cause or exacerbate depression, and individuals with depression may turn to drugs or alcohol to self-medicate.

2. Anxiety: Anxiety is another common mental health issue associated with addiction. Anxiety disorders are characterized by excessive worry and fear, and individuals with anxiety may turn to drugs or alcohol to self-medicate. Substance abuse can worsen anxiety symptoms, leading to a vicious cycle of addiction and mental health issues.

3. Post-Traumatic Stress Disorder (PTSD): PTSD is a mental health disorder that can develop after experiencing or witnessing a traumatic event. Individuals with PTSD may turn to drugs or alcohol to cope with their symptoms, leading to the development of addiction. Similarly, substance abuse can worsen the symptoms of PTSD, leading to a cycle of addiction and mental health issues.

4. Bipolar Disorder: Bipolar disorder is a mental health disorder characterized by extreme mood swings, from periods of high energy and euphoria to periods of depression and hopelessness. Individuals with bipolar disorder are at an increased risk of developing substance abuse issues, and substance abuse can worsen the symptoms of bipolar disorder.

Treatment for Addiction and Mental Health Issues

Effective treatment for addiction and mental health issues must address both conditions concurrently. Dual diagnosis treatment is a comprehensive approach that focuses on treating addiction and mental health disorders simultaneously. Dual diagnosis treatment typically involves a combination of medication-assisted treatment, psychotherapy, and support groups.

1. Medication-Assisted Treatment (MAT): Medication-assisted treatment is an evidence-based approach to treating addiction that involves the use of medications to reduce cravings and withdrawal symptoms. MAT is effective in treating opioid, alcohol, and nicotine addiction, and it can be used in combination with psychotherapy to achieve better outcomes.

2. Psychotherapy: Psychotherapy is an essential component of addiction and mental health treatment. Various psychotherapies, such as cognitive-behavioral therapy (CBT), dialectical behavior therapy (DBT), and motivational interviewing, are effective in treating addiction and mental health issues. Psychotherapy can help individuals identify and address the underlying causes of their addiction and mental health issues and develop healthy coping strategies.

3. Support Groups: Support groups, such as Alcoholics Anonymous (AA) and Narcotics Anonymous (NA), can be an effective tool in treating addiction and mental health issues. Support groups provide a safe and supportive environment where individuals can share their experiences and receive support from others who have been through similar struggles. Support groups can help individuals feel less alone in their recovery journey and provide them with

the motivation and encouragement they need to maintain sobriety.

Challenges in Treating Addiction and Mental Health Issues

Treating addiction and mental health issues simultaneously can be challenging, as each condition can exacerbate the symptoms of the other. Individuals with co-occurring disorders may require more intensive and longer-term treatment to achieve lasting recovery. Additionally, some medications used to treat mental health disorders may have addictive properties, which can complicate treatment.

Stigma surrounding addiction and mental health issues can also be a barrier to effective treatment. Many individuals may feel ashamed or embarrassed about seeking treatment for addiction and mental health issues and may be hesitant to seek help. Stigma can also prevent individuals from accessing quality care and may lead to discrimination and social isolation.

Conclusion

Addiction and mental health issues are closely intertwined, and each condition can exacerbate the symptoms of the other. Effective treatment for addiction and mental health issues must address both conditions simultaneously, and dual diagnosis treatment is the most effective approach. Dual diagnosis treatment typically involves a combination of medication-assisted treatment, psychotherapy, and support groups. However, treating addiction and mental health issues can be challenging, and individuals with co-occurring disorders may require more intensive and longer-term treatment to achieve lasting recovery. Stigma surrounding addiction and mental health issues can also be a barrier to effective treatment, and it is essential to break down these barriers to ensure that individuals can access the care they need to achieve long-term recovery.

This book, "A Comprehensive Overview of Global Challenges," presents an in-depth examination of some of the most pressing issues facing the world today. This book provides a detailed analysis of 15 chapters, covering topics such as climate change, income inequality, discrimination, cybersecurity, financial instability, and many others. Through a multidisciplinary approach, this book explores the complex nature of these challenges and offers potential solutions for addressing them. This book serves as a valuable resource for policymakers, scholars, and anyone interested in gaining a better understanding of the global challenges we face today.

ABOUT THE AUTHOR

Mr. C. P. Kumar is a retired Scientist 'G' from the National Institute of Hydrology, Roorkee, Uttarakhand, India. With a wealth of experience in his field, he has also been practicing alternative healing therapies for several years. He is skilled in Reiki Healing and Chakra Balancing with Pendulum Dowsing, and offers holistic therapy through Emotional Freedom Technique (EFT) for emotional issues. You can email Mr. Kumar at cpkumar@yahoo.com and also visit his Reiki blog at https://reiki-roorkee.blogspot.com/ for more information.